DROPLETS

KNOWN is the manifestation of UNKNOWN,
Know the KNOWN to know UNKNOWN

ANUSHKA KAPSE

Eternal You

Copyright © Anushka Kapse 2020.

The views and opinions expressed in this book are the author's own and the facts are as reported by her, and the publishers are not in any way liable for the same.

All Rights Reserved. No part of this publication may be reproduced, stored in a retrieval system or transmitted, in any form or by any means, electronic, mechanical, photocopying, recording or otherwise, without the prior permission of the publishers.

First Edition : July 2020
ISBN : 9798664918496

Cover Page Photo Courtesy : Mr.Vinod Kapse
Cover Page Design : Mr.Sandesh Ghate
Published By : Eternal You

||Mettañ ca sabba-lokasmim, Manasam bhavaye aparimanam

Uddham adho ca tiriyanca, Asambadham averam asapattam||

Cultivate an all-embracing

mind of love,

For all throughout the universe,

In all its height, depth and breadth-

Love that is untroubled And

beyond hatred or enmity.

*A*cknowledgments

To my loving son, Aditya, who motivates and encourages me. His love and nuggets of insights awestruck me. Thank you for being in my life as my strength.

My deepest appreciation to my dear husband for his boundless energy and enthusiasm for life.

My gratitude to my parents, who offered a higher educational opportunity against all the odds. I am deeply in gratitude for their love and support.

My thanks for constant love and support go to my siblings and my in-laws.

Lastly, to all those spiritual masters, who guided me through their teachings directly and indirectly. I am forever in debt to them.

Dedication

For all the beautiful souls who are standing on the invisible line of Materialism and Spiritualism and keep swinging on both the sides.

And to those who never liked to READ any book but picked this for their LOVE towards ME.

It's dedicated to you all.

Anushka's quark may be a 'Droplet,' but it has the power to cause a Tsunami.

Love n Light

Dr. Trupti Jayin

B.OT, M.A., M.Phil, Clinical Psychologist, Spiritual Life Coach ,Past Life Therapist

*C*ONTENTS

Preface   *10*

1.	*The Lily*	*17*
2.	*The Cube Of Life*	*23*
3.	*Reflection*	*27*
4.	*Passion And Compassion*	*33*
5.	*Blessings*	*37*
6.	*The Garden Of Life*	*41*
7.	*Seen Unseen*	*47*
8.	*The Road*	*53*
9.	*Milk And Salt*	*59*
10.	*TINA*	*63*
11.	*Freedom*	*67*
12.	*Money And Spirituality*	*71*
13.	*Relationships*	*77*
14.	*Love*	*95*
15.	*Cosmic Roots*	*103*
16.	*Himalaya*	*107*
17.	*Pot*	*113*
18.	*Inner Lotus*	*123*

About the Author   *135*

Preface

When my whole being Became an Eye,

I could see YOU.

You were the same LIGHT, My Guide,

My Love, My Life.

I remembered that death has no power to change;

that which has the power to change

is called LOVE.

Be Love - Swami Rama

It was the year 2014; I was driving on a busy Mumbai road, listening to songs and singing along in the privacy of my car.

Ohh, not again.

With intense pain in my heart, I started crying, apparently for no reason. My eyes were raining, and I was not able to see ahead. I stopped the car at the roadside and allowed it to happen.

is going, where all of life is going. And you will be able to feel that this is the only way to be at ease and in harmony with existence, the only way to dissolve yourself into the whole." – Osho

The canvass of my life got broadened and I could see in my mind's eye the deeper aspect of Life. My awareness started expanding and with that, I could draw nourishment from the same soil, detaching myself from unwanted bugs. I started understanding the hidden meaning of my existence, the Love that I am; lighting my life path.

Finally, this is for you O My Priceless LOVE,

"This path towards ABSOLUTE was opened to me because of you, my LOVE. The love within me gave immense pain that my search to get relief began.

It's YOU who invoked my inner beauty and bought me face to face with ABSOLUTE, although in a very torturous manner.

Now on this path, bearing my light, holding your hand and in your light moving ahead to reach closer and closer to INFINITE...

The path is illuminated as I can see and feel with our lights, guiding each other. I know that a time will come when these individual lights will become one and brighten and lighten the path of many others.

We have to keep moving, holding and guiding each other, O My Priceless LOVE."

A single drop from the Sky invokes the excitement of soaking in Rain within us. A single drop is enough to hope, to predict, to prepare, to feel what is on the way.

In this book, there are tiny droplets gathered from my spiritual journey. Even if a single droplet could inspire, motivate, and lead you towards the ocean of INFINITE, my purpose of writing this book is fulfilled.

I suggest you to read each chapter independently. Spend a few minutes or hours or maybe days, thinking on the same.

Preface

It was not 1st time this was happening to me. A few days back, I was standing middle of the highway on the divider and crying, again reason unknown.

Past many months, I was struggling to get over the physical pain I was experiencing in my heart. It was not just a painful feeling but a physical pain that we experience when we are hurt physically. I tried to get relief by doing all sorts of medical tests, but everything seems to be healthy. Even went to a psychologist, but the pain didn't subside. Day after day, it became a struggle to overcome this inner agony.

I was living a perfectly happy life with a family to support and everything at my disposal. But this pain made me think and look at myself from a different perspective. I was struggling to blossom in a soil that has been offered to me, but I guess I was not able to root in that soil fully. In a practical manner, the soil was perfect and there shouldn't be any reason for not rooting in it. But the material wealth and pleasure were not nourishments to my soul. For many years, I was accepting and living as per society's set norms, and it was going right. A sweet family life, satisfying social life, financial security, etc. etc.

Anushka Kapse

What does more one need in life?

But was it so?

It gave me immense pain when I saw how the most sacred and closest relationships function under the influence of societal beliefs and egoism. How the affection, love changes as per approval or disapproval of those in the commanding position. My faith in 'No matter what, Love conquers' was shaken, seeing the conditionality of sharing love and affection. Till the time you function within the set framework, you are accepted, loved. I was observing and understanding that all these things are well accepted and normal way of functioning in the world. It was not OTHERS but my perception towards it was creating inner-conflict.

My thoughts on spirituality, awareness, social work were not well received and mostly ignored, which created confusion in my mind. Since childhood, I was a self-reliant and self-confident girl, but now my self-confidence was shaken, my inner dialogue and thoughts were creating doubts on my capacity. Many times, you feel lonely, even when you are surrounded by a crowd. This inner turmoil was not seen outside as I have to project myself in

Preface

a certain way (societal conditioning), and I was a good actor as nobody could even get a hint as to what is happening with me.

Unable to bear the heart pain, I shared it with my close friend, who guided me to do a Past Life Regression healing session.

This guidance was a turning point.

At this point, my other friend gifted me a spiritual book. I read it immediately. Before finishing that book, more books were already in line for me, sent by the universe as coincidently those books used to flash in front of me either in newspapers or on the e-commerce sites..

Those were the books where I can see the reflection of my thoughts. For a few months, I was reading like a thirsty crow, quenching my thirst for knowledge. My self-confidence started coming back. I started rooting myself in the Light of those whom I used to worship as Enlightened beings' Swami Vivekananda,' 'Buddha,' 'Saint Gyaneshwar.' I was happy to find my reflection of thoughts in their teachings and getting some relief from heart pain, but still, something was missing.

I decided to try PLRT as suggested by my friend, and so enrolled myself for the workshop. This opportunity opened me to my inner self in the most beautiful way.

The beautiful Lotus flower received by 'Lord Buddha' in a deep trance has engraved on my mind forever, asking me to rise 'ABOVE' just like a Lotus. The blessing opened many dimensions for me. For the next two years, I continued to read many spiritual books written by various masters, undergone more PLR sessions, learned different healing modalities, cultivated habit of meditation & yoga, attended powerful workshops of living yogi's, experimented with gathered knowledge to draw wisdom, traveled to my favorite mountain Himalaya.

My thought process and experiences and messages received during meditation or spiritual session points towards something my conscious mind was not able to fully integrate, mainly because my immediate surrounding did not support it and I wanted their approval. But I continued and persisted my Sadhana only keeping my focus on Lotus.

*"Never be bothered about anything else, only one thing – one thing is the whole religion, and that is **AWARENESS**, and then you will be able to see where your life*

◆ DROPLET ONE

The Lily

You are the fearless guardian

of Divine Light.

So come, return to the root of

the root of your Soul- Rumi

The womb of lily (Futaba Barbados), when it emerges from its source, carries four flower buds inside it as ONE. As it starts growing slowly, it starts separating individual buds. When the time comes to blossom in beautiful lily flower entirely, all four flowers turn towards four directions giving sufficient space to each other to expand and blossom to its full potential.

Amazing, isn't it?

Individual growth honoring the needs of others is such a unique quality...

The infinite Creation has come out of one single SOURCE manifested in millions of forms.

Consider these flowers as human beings originated from one single source, each wanting to blossom fully...

Is it not possible?

Surely it is, if each one understands the needs of others and honors it just like nature does. After all, humans are 'nature' too...

But why a plant like 'Lily' can do this and so-called 'evolved' human race finds it difficult?

The Lily

The plant has connected to it's 'ROOTS,' which provides nourishment and strength. Without these roots there is no existence for this plant.

The human race has come far away from its 'ROOTS,' it's 'SOURCE'. .They have deprived themselves of the nourishment and inner strength provided by SOURCE.

Once they feel connected, they will see the ONENESS of CREATION, and the endless struggle of life will get dissolved in the soothing touch of CREATOR.

Consider these flowers as 'Religions,' it's possible for each religion to blossom fully, IF and ONLY IF they all remain connected to 'SOURCE' as then, they will understand, it's 'ME' expressed in 'OTHER.'

Will the meaning of 'Love' change if we say 'Ishque' or 'Ti Amo' or 'Prem' or 'Aishiteru' or 'Wo Ie ni'?. It will invoke the same feeling within you if you understand it, else it's mere another word.

The problem today is everybody says different words for the same thing without truly understanding it ... That is why so much violence, hatred, anger towards other religions, sects are seen everywhere.

The world suffers because it is more concerned about the 'word' than practicing its' meaning.'

I came across this beautiful poetic perception of the universality of God by these three legendary poets in Urdu literature.

Ghalib(1797 -1869)

Iqbal(1877-1938)

and Faraz(1931-2008)

Ghalib started it in the 18th century.

झहीद, शराब पिने दे मस्जिद में बैठं कर

या वो जगह बता, जहां खुदा नहीं ।

"Zahid, sharaab peene de masjid mein baith kar, Ya wo jagah bataa, jahaan Khuda nahin"

Translation:

Let me drink in a mosque; or tell me the place where there is no God.'

Allama Iqbal was not convinced. He decided to reply about half a century later, his poetic reply to Ghalib.

The Lily

मस्जिद खुदा का घर है, पीने कि जगह नहीं

काफिर के दिल में जा, वहां खुदा नहीं ।

"Masjid Khuda ka Ghar hai, peene ki jagah nahin, Kaafir ke dil mein jaa, wahaan Khuda Nahin"

Translation:

The mosque is the abode of God, not a place to drink. Go to the heart of a non-believer because there God is not.

Faraz had the last word. (Later half of the 19th century) .

काफिर के दिल से आया हुं मैं ये देख कर फरझ,

खुदा मौजूद है वहां, पर उसें पता नहीं ।

"Kaafir ke dil se aaya hun, main ye dekh kar Faraz, Khuda maujood hai wahaan, par usey pata Nahin"

Translation:

I have returned from the heart of the disbeliever, and I have observed that God is present in his heart too, but he just doesn't know it.

How beautifully they expressed the universality of God. Swami Ramkrishna Paramhansa has practiced Hindu, Muslim and Christan religion during his lifetime and declared that,

As out of one Gold, ornaments of various forms are made; so it is the same God that is worshipped by different nations under different names and different forms .-

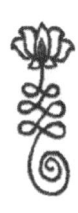

Swami Ramkrishna Paramhansa

● *DROPLET TWO*

The Cube of Life

'I' as came from EGO,

a product of Individual Mind,

'I' as came from AWARENESS,

a product of Universal Mind.

Human life as a journey from

अहं to अहम् ब्रह्मास्मि

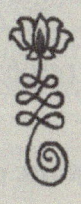

When we achieve mastery over life obstacles, no matter how complicated the situation is, we can solve it, as now you have learned the fundamentals of life..

Know that twists and turns of life will help you to reach your ultimate goal.

Be AWARE of it...ACCEPT it

⬛ *DROPLET THREE*

Reflection

**The BEAUTY
you see in ME,
Is a REFLECTION
of YOU**

***O**nce the Sky decided to explore the universe, so he started moving around...*

He looked down and saw a barren land....

'Ohhh, I am so dry!'

He felt sad.

As he turned another side, he saw a beautiful meadow,

'Alas, I am so green and beautiful!'

He felt good.

A few miles ahead and he spotted a river flowing. When he looked into the river, he saw himself blue.

'hmmm...'

He became confused.

Nevertheless, he decided to continue, and soon, he came across an ocean. As he saw into it, he found a vast reflection of different colors in it. Now he became more confused.

'Am I dry or green or blue or small or big????'

So many questions.

Reflection

Then he started searching something bigger than the ocean to look into it.

But he couldn't find anything.

What to do?

He became still and thought,

'All the while I was looking into something outside to find myself, let's now look into ME to find ME.'

So he turned inward.

*He found **NOTHING**...*

He became more still...more still.... and in that stillness, he found a Ray of Light passing through it. He just got hold of it and moved inward...

'Oh, so I am this huge-with no beginning and no end.

*I am the universe to which I was looking into...finally, I found **MYSELF in ME.'***

Many times we see ourselves as per others' reflection of us, ...so it is crucial to know into whom you see your reflection as that reflection depends upon other's perceptions, capacity to look through, and expectations from YOU...

Anushka Kapse

In the stillness of mind, you will find a mirror right inside you...

It is this mirror that will show you YOUR true reflection without any discrimination.

It's a scientific fact that the amount of light reflected by an OBJECT, and how it is reflected, is highly dependent upon the smoothness or texture of the SURFACE. When surface imperfections are smaller (as in the case of a mirror), virtually all of the light is reflected equally. However, on the convoluted surface, the light gets reflected in all directions.

The light of our soul (OBJECT) will be reflected depending on the smoothness of our mind (SURFACE). The more still and stain-free is the mind; the perfect is the reflection of that supreme light.

Saint Nivrutinath was Guru of Saint Dnyaneshwar. Below is the extract of dialogue/ [1] between them when Saint Dynaneshwar had Self-Realization.

अरे अरे ज्ञाना झालासी पावन ।

---

[1] *English translation of above dialogue is sourced.*

● *DROPLET FOUR*

Passion and Compassion

Passion CREATES...

Dispassion DESTROYS

Between these two lies a LIFE

that need to be lived with

COMPASSION.

Passion keeps you 'Attached' to your Creation viz relationship, money, fame, success, etc.

Dispassion makes you 'Detached' to the passion, thus helping you overcome the apathy or suffering it brings along.

Does that mean one should not love or strive for success or fame in fear of getting attached?

Does detachment mean keeping oneself away from a worldly affair?

Whenever one creates something, the ego mind makes him attached to Creation by instilling belief system, invoking various feelings; either positive or negative, as Ego wants to sustain itself. The more you identify yourself with it, the stronger it becomes. Ego hides behind opinions that appear authentic – our attachment to descriptions of our identity. Thus the wheel of 'Maya' sustains through YOU identifying with your false self. Passion always brings along with it apathy or suffering.

Detachment comes with Awareness of our True Nature that lies beyond False Ego.

Detachment is separation from attachment. It is the separation of Ego from Higher Self.

When 'I' from EGO and 'I' from higher consciousness gets separated, detachment happens.

Then even though the Ego mind remains in a worldly setting, the higher self remains detached to imprints of Ego Mind.

Detachment is not running away from your life purpose or dharma or being indifferent towards other's emotions.

The root of detachment lies in 'Divine Love.'

When you experience Divine LOVE, you understand that you are in everyone, and everyone is in you, so to whom you will attach?

The radius of the heart of a truly detached person is unlimited. It includes everything and everybody with the same love and compassion without any judgment.

A truly detached person is as strong as a mountain and as soft as a flower.

Anushka Kapse

Detachment without compassion is like a Body without Soul,

Flower without fragrance,

Practice detachment with Compassion and

Experience the beauty of living.

◆DROPLET FIVE

Blessings

Divine's help is there for all-

for each, the benefit is

proportionate to his

RECEPTIVITY and SINCERITY –

Mother Mirra

Anushka Kapse

The cool breeze of the evening got mesmerizing fragrance of Nishigandha flower along with it through the open window. But the next day morning, as the wind changed its direction, I couldn't enjoy that fragrance. But since I have experienced the scent an evening before, I knew where to go. I went closer to the flower and enjoyed the same mesmerizing fragrance again. The flower with fragrance was always THERE. But this time, I didn't depend on the breeze to bring that fragrance to me because I knew the SOURCE of it, so I simply turned myself in the right direction.

The universe is full of abundance, and the Creator's blessings are everywhere. We enjoy his blessings in the form of fulfilling relationships, good health, wealth, etc.

Many times under the influence of wants and desires, we endlessly chase happiness in a materialistic world that is ever-changing and forget the everlasting divine blessing around.

When we recognize the blessings in our life, however small or big those might be, we carry gratitude in our heart, and this gratitude makes us tuned to divine blessings.

Blessings

Whatever you desire for yourself in life, make yourself TUNED to it just as the way we tune to a particular channel of radio by adjusting the frequency to listen to the music of our choice. A song is already playing there for everyone, but whoever tunes to that frequency, enjoys it.

There is always a blessing of **'LOVE'**....*tune into it*

There is always a blessing of **'PEACE'**....*tune into it*

There is always a blessing of **'SUCCESS'**.....*tune into it*

There is always a blessing of **'HAPPINESS'**....*tune into it*

and so on.

If you feel God is not showering his blessings on you, think again, and

Check...

Check, if any of window of your mind is closed that is not allowing you to experience blessings or

Check, if you have tuned yourself at correct frequency ? or

Check, if you depend on some external source to take you to blessings?

The winds of grace are always blowing, but you have to raise the sail.-

Swami Ramkrishna Paramhansa

◆ *DROPLET SIX*

<u>**The Garden of Life**</u>

All Differences in this world

are of degree, and not of kind

because oneness is the

the secret of everything.-

Swami Vivekanand

While creating a beautiful garden, a wise gardner knows that the garden will attract both butterflies and bugs on which he has little or no control. Expecting only Butterflies (Good) and not bugs(Bad) is foolishness. As wise gardner is aware and accepts this fact, he will try to find out ways that will minimize EFFECT of these poisonous snakes, worms, bugs, etc. keeping in mind worm and bugs are equally important for the health of his garden to maintain an ecosystem...Maybe he will keep some birds that will add beauty and whose fear will keep away snakes or worms that create havoc. He will design a self-sufficient, co-dependent atmosphere to keep his garden beautiful and healthy. Once he learns how to do this in one place, he can then go on repeating the same on other barren lands, becoming the Creator of his happiness.

Nature comprises of a variety of things...trees, shrubs, bushes, creepers of different sizes, colors and characteristics. Some gives us food, some flowers, some shadows, some protection, some visual treat and of course oxygen. This diversity is necessary to keep balance in nature. What would have happened if everywhere the same type of environment is seen???

The Garden of Life

It would have been monotonous and harmful. Isn't it??

Diversity brings joy in our lives, if and only if diversity is accepted and respected by everyone.

Nature does this perfectly. There is no conflict of variety in the environment. Each n Every Creation has a role to play in the garden.

But what happens to this diversity when it comes to humans? After all, a human is also nature's creation. Our human life is a beautiful garden. Each type of individual is vital to keep this garden balanced, serene, healthy, and happy. Just imagine what will happen if everybody has the same qualities, same behavior, same traits, same minds. How boring, isn't it?

Variety adds beauty and excitement in living. Different shades of thoughts, different shapes of physical appearance, different ways of actions add so much wisdom and harmony in our life. Since eons, there is not much difference in human motivation and inspirations. Money, Power, Sex, Love, Freedom in one or the other shades continue to inspire humankind. Notice how everyone reacts differently to the seemingly same situation. If you become the observer of the situation than an active participator, you will gain many life insights. But as we attach ourselves to people or circumstances, we miss on those valuable drops of wisdom.

Every relation brings something to an individual's life. Some carry love, some care, some teach us lessons, some friendships, some teach us life values, some guide us, some bring stress, but it will bring something. Our mind chooses those who satisfy our needs and makes life comfortable, labeling others as troublesome.

Learn and try to accept the diversity of characteristics of everyone around to get balance in life.

Embracing the differences with an awareness that it is all but a different manifestation of the same SOURCE will keep everything in balance, and human beings will enjoy more content and frictionless life.

The Garden of Life

***H**uman being wants to control everything. This need for exercising power to control others, bring misery to himself and to others. But how much little this INTELLIGENT creature can do .Just try to separate petals of a bud to turn it into a flower...can you do it without spoiling the bud??*

We can't make a bud bloom externally. It takes its own time to get formed fully in shape and size. The changes are INTERNAL...

Once it's fully ready, slowly it starts opening up with its speed. We can't speed up the process by an external force. Slow or fast as per nature; ***IT WILL BLOOM.***

Every bud has its rate and time to bloom. However best care and nourishments you provide, it will flower in its flowering season only. It is in genes of the plant, what kind of flower or fruit it will have. Externally we can just provide the right environment and nourishment suitable for blossom.

An apple tree will never give you mango, however the best care you take. And if you get disappointed that your wish of mangoes is not fulfilled, then you won't even enjoy the Apples provided by the tree as per its nature. What is the fault of the apple tree if it gave you apples and not mangoes???

Most of the time, parents want Mangoes from their Apple of eyes and get disappointed. Each child has its own pace for coming to blossom. Some have early blossom, and some take a lot of time. Parents get anxious and try to forcibly bloom the tender bud, which may not have developed yet. In the process, they damage the bud beyond repair. As a parent, provide a suitable environment and nourishment for kids to bloom all by themselves. It's a natural process. You have to be patient and supportive and focus on your role of providing strong roots/foundation; rest all will happen automatically.

Prepare yourself to accept if he/she turns out to be a different blossom than you wished for.. Afterall, they have come through you, but they are not you.
A flower does not think of competing with the flower next to it. It just blooms. : Unknown

◆ *DROPLET SEVEN*

<u>Seen Unseen</u>

Reality of Things is hidden

in the Realm of

Unseen –

Hamza Yusuf

Anushka Kapse

What do you see in Milk?

Milk as it is, or Curd or Butter?

An ignorant person will say,

'It's only Milk.' and reject all other produce, and he will enjoy 'Milk.'

Good enough !!!

But a wise one will first accept MILK as it is and then apply his wisdom to find if he can do more with MILK. This acquired wisdom will make him do experiments, execute necessary steps, and manifest BUTTER.

In this world, a person who is fully immersed in materialistic pursuit will see the world entirely through physical senses. He will enjoy the world through 'MILK' viz food, drinks, money, sex, success, worldly objects, etc. He will reject the existence of 'BUTTER' or simply remains happy with his MILK.

Milk represents your bodily and worldly desires &

Butter is your ultimate nature hidden inside you.

Seen Unseen

Your capacity to see things beyond your physical senses gives you the ability to find more profound aspects of life and thus enjoy the benefits.

An ignorant will ask,

' What is wrong if I like to enjoy Milk which is readily available and known to me than to run behind butter which I don't even know if exists?

Is it not better to enjoy Known than the Unknown? '

Hmmmm...valid question.

You are feeling very hungry. You ate to your stomach full and felt happy.

You are feeling thirsty. You drank your heart full and felt happy.

You satisfied your sexual urges and felt happy.

You could spend money to fulfill your desires and felt happy.

Now, will you take that next bite of your most favorite food when your stomach is full or drink that favorite drink or feel the urge to have sex when your bodily needs are satisfied?

Chances are you will feel disgusting towards those things you enjoy through your senses once it is fulfilled at that time.

Your capacity to enjoy food, drink, sex, success, money diminishes as you grow older.

The physical, mental, emotional needs keep on changing at different stages of life.

Need-based happiness lasts till the time of your next hunger (bodily, mental, emotional), for those needs will arise again and seek satisfaction. If you can't fulfil those needs, you will experience unhappiness, bitterness, sadness. So day after day, years after years one is busy in satisfying those Needs which are temporarily permanent.

Sometimes you know that there is Butter in Milk, but still, you want to enjoy' Milk 'as you are not yet ready to undergo a transformation which needs churning to happen, you don't want to come out of the comfort zone of life.

But the one who understands the ever-changing and perishable nature of MILK will then start searching for Butter.

Becoming aware of this Truth is 1ˢᵗ step towards more permeant happiness.

After acquiring the required wisdom and practicing the same consistency in a disciplined manner will take you closer to' Butter,' which is a non-perishable and permanent form of Milk.

Milk to Curd to Butter is a non-reversible process. It's a one-way journey.

Spiritual transformation is too non-reversible; once it occurs, it stays forever.

Let the churning happen. Let the Butter be experienced.

As fragrance abides in flower,

As reflection is within the mirror,

So does your Lord abides within you,

Why search for him without? -

Guru Nanak

Anushka Kapse

Your Insight

DROPLET EIGHT

The Road

It's your Road and yours alone,

Others may walk it with you,

But no one can walk it for you -

Rumi

Anushka Kapse

A human being is a social animal. It needs relationships to feel connected. This connectedness is not necessarily with only other human being but with any other living entity or skill or work or cause or anything which gives happiness and fulfillment. But the most basic and essential way to feel connected is experienced through our relationships where we can express ourselves and receive something in return. The exchange happens to form a bond of care, affection, and love.

When a road is getting constructed to connect places, lots of activities happen.

Why is this road required?

How to do?

What will it connect?

What benefit will it give? etc.

If this road is going through already captured land, then a lot of resistance will be there to get it constructed. Once actual work begins, lots of labor and material are required. Work will be done under the experienced guidance of people who knows road construction. The road is carved using various construction tools,

The Road

blasts dynamite. When entirely done, it's now convenient to travel on a familiar path easily as and when required. The chances of getting lost are minimal if you are a frequent user of this road and Nil if you are Creator of this road.

Every human being can construct a road of his own to connect with other realities of life. As with physical road, when the invisible road of love, care, trust, affection is required to built between relationships, one needs to overcome debris of misunderstanding, Ego, insecurities, envy, etc. If we genuinely want to make this road, then we will take efforts and pain to remove this debris and pave our desired way of fulfilling relationships.

When a Sadhak (seeker) wants to build a road to connect to other Realities of cosmos, he too has to clear the clutter of worldly desires, ego, attachments, materialism before he could see the path.

When he starts decluttering, he gets resistance from his physical body and mind. Still, if he continues with determination, slowly, the connection begins opening up. Through that connection, one can get glimpses of what is lying beyond, But a sadhak must continue to build his road...This point is crucial as sadhak may get lost in the sights if he doesn't know where exactly he needs to be connected, and he may go on scattering here and there without proper direction.

At such juncture, if he gets guidance from souls who have already established such connections is of great help. The knowledge they impart will help sadhak to connect his road with the already established path, and then the onward journey becomes easy.

The other way is just to go on doing the trial and error method, experiment, and construct your road. Here too, it is vital to get the right knowledge by whatever source one can.

The Road

The road such created then itself becomes the established path for others to connect to. But without proper knowledge, the chances of getting road damaged are incredibly high, and walking on such a route will not take you to the desired destination.

Whatever method one chooses to opt for, the invisible road, thus made out of sheer dedication, devotion, and knowledge, will be open to sadhak to experience other realities.

He then can choose to run, walk, or simply stroll on this road as per his wish. He becomes the Guide to many others who may wish to connect to his path to reach the final destination or wants to construct his road.

Build your road to divine connection and experience the beauty within.

Anushka Kapse

Your Insight

DROPLET NINE

Milk and Salt

The meeting of two personalities

is like the contact of two

chemical substances;

if there is any reaction,

both are transformed.-

Carl Jung

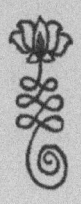

Anushka Kapse

T*here was a famous Hindustani classical music Goddess who was the ex-wife of another Hindustani classical music Demigod. The supreme being had bestowed on them the blessing of music, which is one of the most potent means to experience the bliss.*

Both the singers achieved that bliss - one through DEVOTION and another through PASSION...

One found it in the internal world, another in the external world ...One in solitude and another in applaud.

However, together they were disaster just like Milk and Salt.

The human Ego superseded their love for music. They can not cultivate love towards each other.

It's so strange that one can love the means of happiness unconditionally but can't love another life unconditionally.

Whoever discovers the divinity within, with whatever means, will know that 'There are no others', so there is no need to ACCEPT others...

Milk and Salt

Everything is You and You are Everything.

Both the legendries had their desires to be fulfilled...The need for larger than life experience through music drawn him to become people's musician. Being prominent 'Rajas' quality, he needed to be surrounded by people; the materialistic world was his playground...

The pain she got from the relationship had triggered her 'Satvik' quality and pushed her in solitude to realize her true self...she internalized her grief and found solace in Devotion. It was said that her music was so divine that when she used to do riyaz in solitude, divinity used to descend in the room, and it used to fill with a heavenly fragrance.

Milk and Salt have their individual and unique existence.

Both are equally important parts of food. But unlike Milk-Sugar combination, Milk-Salt duo is a disaster.

Milk-Sugar duo keeps their individuality intact while creating a new, more beautiful output.

Milk-Salt loses its individuality, creating a disastrous output that is not usable by itself.

However, if an external ingredient is added, it can then be transformed into something usable, but in the process, both of them have to lose their existence entirely.

If, unfortunately, you are in Milk-Salt type relationship, try adding external ingredients like 'mutual respect, nonjudgment, acceptance,' and you will notice you have created a new relationship which is more comfortable and adjustable.

Sustain reaction and

Bring transformation.

◆ DROPLET TEN

<u>***TINA***</u>

You can't stop the waves,

but you can learn to Surf. –

Joseph Goldstein

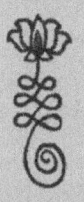

Many times a person accepts the things to maintain harmony in life... It's the 'peace-loving' quality of that person who tries to balance his environment. The mind takes pride in this quality of his, which many don't possess... but many times in this process knowingly and unknowingly, he accepts the things out of TINA (There Is No Alternative) effect than out of pure love of acceptance and understanding.

In such a case, imprints of disappointment n hurt get imbibed on a deeper layer of the mind. On the surface level, everything seems fine as your mind loves to maintain the 'peace-loving' tag. But if one goes on deeper levels of consciousness by delayering, he will find these imprints of disappointment and hurt.

Your conscious mind creates the illusion that everything is excellent, and this is how the world works as that soothes the living experience. The person can spend his entire life in this way as what he wants is harmony and peace in life without realizing his own soul's need as he is afraid to face it...Soul searching means rearranging, breaking old patterns, and recreating new patterns in alignment with your soul. This may bring many turns n twists in physical life, and one may not be yet ready to accept those out of fear and his own physical and emotional needs... Working on needs in the known world for the sake of the unknown world is something beyond the mind's reach.. so the cycle continues... The imprints remain dormant on the deep recess of mind waiting to be healed so that his soul breath easy.

Acceptance with the TINA effect might bring peace in external existence, but your inner world remains in turmoil.

Acceptance with a deeper understanding that comes with soul searching will bring permanent peace and harmony in the external and internal world.

AWARENESS and ACCEPTANCE together bring FREEDOM.

Anushka Kapse

Your Insight

◆ *DROPLET ELEVEN*

Freedom

The fly that touches honey,

cannot use its wings;

so too the soul that clings to

spiritual sweetness ruins

it's freedom and hinder

contemplation.

– Sri Aurobindo

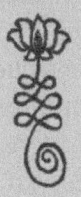

Anushka Kapse

***H**ave you ever heard or seen fishes trying hard to live on the ground?*

They are happy to live in the waters.

Have you ever heard or seen ground creatures like an ant, rat, animals are practicing to fly in the Sky?

They are happy to live on the ground.

Have you ever heard or seen a bird being unhappy because he couldn't fly in space?

They are very much at peace, soaring in the Sky.

But you must have heard almost every time that a human being is trying to be happy in his physical existence.

Why can't he be at peace with his surroundings?

Is it because a human being has the capacity to soar beyond earth, water, sky existence?

Somewhere deep inside, he knows it's the strength of roaming freely in this universe. In ignorance, he searches for happiness in immediate surroundings but fails... Only an individual whose awareness is heightened, then search for eternal happiness beyond physicality, and once it's found, he is in bliss at his earthly existence. It's the capacity of the human mind which can go beyond its physical surroundings makes him distinct species.

Don't let go of this precious human life behind temporary physical happiness, soar high, release your true potential to be a human being- an image of that magnificent cosmos.

The soul always wants to experience freedom, which is its eternal nature but its human mind, which creates many illusions and hinders the soul experience. It's through mind's gateway one can connect to a higher self, but many times the imprints on mind blocks these gateways. The more a clear mind, the more close you are towards your higher self, which is the source of wisdom. The imprints on your mind are like stains on the cloth. Once you are clear of these stains, you can see the clean cloth, and now you have to work on making this cloth transparent to see beyond.

Another way is to tear this cloth entirely and merge. Many times for ascended masters, it is required to come in earthly form for guiding humanity. Such times, although they are in physical form, but with a transparent cloth on their mind, they can see BEYOND effortlessly. Their consciousness is universal, and they can access the past, present, and future. A truly enlightened being won't get entangled in Siddhi's, which he has bestowed with during spiritual heights...

Siddhi's are a by-product and not the destination of the seeker.

The one who gets attracted by the spiritual powers won't reach the ultimate height of spiritual bliss, spiritual union.

As Osho said,

'Responsibility is the first step towards Freedom.'

Be free :)

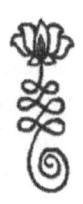

DROPLET TWELVE

<u>Money and Spirituality</u>

Money is the worst discovery of human life.

But it is the most trusted material to test human nature. –

Buddha

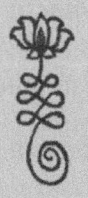

Money has become the most widely used and understood (misunderstood) language of the planet earth.

Money doesn't have value for itself.

It is neutral.

The value is to the HAPPINESS you draw from things, from Desires, from Needs for whose fulfillment money is used.

So the value of money will change from individual to individual depending on his perception towards the importance of needs, desire, things he wishes to use the money on. HAPPINESS may be temporary and EGOISTIC, but it's valuable to the individual. It is a perception that gives value to money.

Suppose you like to purchase a flower, say lotus...as you perceive it as an object of your happiness, you spent money on it; somebody else finds it ridiculous to spent money on a flower as he sees it just as a perishable thing and not as HAPPINESS.

Cumulative perception of people towards certain things makes them pricy such as diamond, gold, certain brands. Its value is the output of people's egoistic self-worth, which they boast using money.

Money and Spirituality

In the modern world, an individual's value is based on their earning capacity. The work which fetches money is respected and valued, but the hard work put in the work which does not give tangible and monetary benefit is considered valueless or neglected or not even acknowledged. That is why our society is patriarchy as it's a male member of the family who is a provider, and mothers' contributions or work is often neglected or on the mercy of approval and appreciation by another gender.

With money comes the power and Ego's need to control others. It is this aspect which has made feminine in the modern world to raise their voice and come out of the clutches of patriarchy who uses money power to control another gender. The need for financial independence which today's women seek has come from the suppression and control exerted by another gender due to money. Our education is only meant to give the power to earn money. The more academically educated you are, the more are your chances to get hefty cheques. A human being is finding security in money than in a relationship or another human being.

The approach of independence is limited to financial independence only.

Does financial freedom offer 'Freedom'?

Freedom to express,

Freedom to live life on your own terms.

For the majority of women, the answer will be NO.

The importance of any work is decided by the amount of money it fetches. The work, such as social work where one doesn't get monetary benefit is by and large considered as the work to be done in free time or after retirement.

As Osho said, "Money seems to be the greatest obsession in the world. Money seems to be the greatest madness in the world. We go on selling our lives and collecting pebbles; we call it money. One day we simply disappear and the money is left here. And the life that you wasted in collecting that money could have been used in a more creative way. It could have become a song, a dance; it could have become a prayer, a meditation; it could have become a realization of truth, freedom... but you missed."

Money and Spirituality

Earning money is not wrong, and one must fulfill its duty of 'Artharjan' as a part of his dharma. An artist creates an Art and earns his livelihood, name, and fame; a similar way, a competent person creates wealth using the power of his intellect. If a person has skill and knack to generate money, he must do it. But this generated money then gets accumulated in the hands of those who then use it to exploit others either knowingly or unknowingly. The problem arises when the need becomes greed, earning more money only to fulfill worldly desires and buy more comforts to prove one's superiority over others.

A wise person will use his skill to create more opportunities for others, helping the economy and society to grow. They will seek individual growth with the growth of others associated with them.

The accumulated wealth, when gets distributed on causes that plague our society, will give spiritual value to the money. It's a powerful tool if used in the right direction.

Experience the power of this tool by detaching yourself with it. When you no more feel the need to possess the things money can buy, your earning will become an offering. The tool will manifest by itself for you to be used more efficiently.

Money is like love;

it kills slowly and painfully the one

who withholds it,

and enlivens the other

who turns it on his fellow man.

- Kahlil Gibran

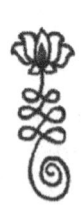

DROPLET THIRTEEN

Relationships

Man's law changes with his understanding of man.

Only the law of spirit remain always the same.-

Crow

Why is that we can love CREATOR but fail to love CREATION?

We even love CREATOR selectively with our belief system and identities, then what is this CREATION to whom we will love unconditionally?

It's our conditioned mind and belief system that makes us behave in a certain way in relationships. This is particularly more evident in the way Marital relationships are handled.

If you do a deep search in the most conflicting relationship, you will find the reason of conflict lies in the mental conditioning. In any given situation, the output would have been different if the relation shared has different conditioning. It's not about the relationship but the prejudiced and conditioned approach towards that relationship, which causes the conflict.

The most challenging relationships in our lives are there to teach us some deep insight required for soul evolvement. Human minds don't learn through good situations. It seeks pleasure and happiness but will learn life lessons only when it is shaken, stirred, and hurt.

Relationships

Somebody said so truly,

Happiness expands us,

Pain deepens us.

Both are necessary for soul evolvement. The heart opens to embrace others when we are happy and expands it's radius of inclusiveness. In pain, we connect to deeper recesses of our mind, which otherwise lies hidden or dormant. In order to get the release from the pain, we search for solutions-externally and then internally. The internal search will take you to connect deeper aspects of your being, finding your self.

If you take an in-depth and unbiased look at your life situations, you will notice repetitive types of incidents, happening through seemingly difficult people, whose lessons will be almost similar. Whether it is to learn honesty, patience, tolerance, love, letting go, detachment, acceptance, overcoming fears, or any other, till the time you don't learn that lesson thoroughly, situations and events will repeat itself using different relationships over lifetimes.

The energy which has created during such events among individuals will leave karmic imprints-positive or negative on the soul, which then becomes the basis of your future lifetimes till such time that there is a bond of neutrality gets created among participating individuals.

Know that all our relationships viz our biological family, our marital family, friends, or any other with whom we share our lives, were with you from many lifetimes. Depending on the type of lesson you and they choose to learn in the current lifetime, and the kind of energy you both are carrying among yourself will decide the closeness or type of relationship equation. Suppose you have to learn the lesson of unconditional love, and you and other soul has agreed to help each other in this lesson. For many lifetimes, both these souls might have shared close relationships to learn 'Love,' as it's easy to love your own blood and flesh. Later they might choose a relationship where they are not connected by blood but by dharma. However, when you are born here, as amnesia happens, you are ruled by your mind and gathered a belief system, which creates many new imprints in relationships, adding to already existing ones. Only when you are aware and rooted

Relationships

in 'Oneness' of Creation, you shall be able to entirely remove or transform those negative imprints, overriding the conditioning of your mind.

Our relationships are the opportunities given to us to evolve, to grow, to learn. It's the unsaid contract between individuals who decides to help each other to evolve.

If you happen to start loving the Creation, under the disguise of that troublemaker's face, you will find the loving divine soul smiling at you unconditionally.

Anushka Kapse

The concept of marriage is formed to experience the union of 2 individuals in body, mind, and spirit. Every concept is developed to give us experience and prepare for that ultimate union we call by various names of 'Nirvana' 'Liberation,' 'Enlightenment,' "Shunya' '....

Each human being has male and female energies within. The MALE energy is of logic, analysis, assertiveness, courage, freedom, independence, and FEMALE energy is of nourishment, care, creativity, intuition, feelings, empathy....

It's not the physical GENDER but the degree of these energies within us that determines our behavior or handling capacity of any given situation in the physical world. So there are many MALE who have dominant qualities of care, affection more than logic and courage... Similarly, there are many FEMALES who are governed by more of the male energy of logic than care, tenderness. When a human being balances these both energies perfectly, we move towards ultimate union. To give a glimpse of how it feels to be ONE, the concept of marriage might have been started, as then the individuals can form a bond of Love, Devotion, Surrender, to reach that ultimate experience of ONENESS. One who ascends from the physical union of 2 bodies lives in a continuous bliss. But due to the influence of our mind, lifetime after lifetime, human beings struggle to balance this male-female or yin-yang energy and reach the ULTIMATE. It's with the repeated circle of life-death we learn to balance the same and ascend to higher dimensions beyond the physical world.

Relationships of Love are more potent to offer you evolvement as it's through relationships you learn how to care, how to love, how to surrender, how to devote oneself.

However, with society's modernization, marriage has become more like an arrangement than the experience of Love, affection, and bonding. Furthermore, having multiple relationships has become an acceptable trend. Falling in and out of relationships is as easy as opening and closing an account.

When a union happens between two individuals, either on a physical, emotional, or mental level, there is energy exchange happening between these two individuals. Both take in other's energy fields within IN.

Anushka Kapse

When you are with multiple partners either simultaneously or one at a time, you are taking in other partner's energy within you, which is becoming part of you, creating deep imprints. The various kind of energy imprints creates deeper and deeper energy entanglement within you, affecting your energy field.

Is it not wise to ask yourself what is the basis of such a union that has such a deep impact?

There is a beautiful story narrated by Om Swamiji in 'Bhaj Govindam' as follows:

"Once a sadhu was roaming in a village for alms. This village was new for him. He randomly knocks on a door. This house was of a prostitute. The prostitute opens the door and sees a radiant sadhu standing on her door. The Sadhu sees a stunningly beautiful women in front of him and smitten by her beauty, he forgets her Dharma as a Sadhu.

He says, 'I don't want alms of food, if you want to give something, then give me your Swaroop (form).'

Relationships

The prostitute thinks, 'what a radiant sadhu he is. How can he deviate from his path? I am not understanding if he is testing me or God is testing me or through me, god is testing him?'

She replies, 'Maharaj, I am menstruating, please come after a week, I will keep my swaroop ready for you.'

Sadhu becomes happy and leaves.

She goes inside house and tells her mother, 'Mata, I shall be in my room for 7 days. I will not take food, will have only water. Please give me silver pots and silk cloths. When sadhu will come, send him to me.'

Mother arranges everything without thinking much.

The women calls a barber and asks him to cut her long lustorous hair and put those hairs in one of the silver pots and cover it with silk cloth.

In another silver pot she puts her solid waste .

In third pot she puts her urine.

She then put her fingers in mouth and omits and put the omit in 4th pot.

For seven days, she didn't take bath nor does cleans her cloth. Whatever dirt comes out, she puts it in another silver pot.

The sadhu who was completely taken over by lust knocks on her door after a week excitedly, dreaming of fulfilling his desire. Her mother opens the door and tells him that for entire week her daughter locked herself in the room and waiting for him. The sadhu become totally aroused by lust and hurriedly enters the room. He gets surprised to see a women under a veil and many silver pots covered with silk cloth.

He says, 'I am here. Give me my alms.'

The women replies, 'Maharaj, you have asked for my 'Swaroop', my true form.. I have kept it ready for you. Pl pick up the silk cloths on those pots, you will know my Swaroop.'

Astonished, sadhu lifts the cover of 1st pot and sees hair inside. He didn't understand anything. Then he picks up cloth from 2nd, 3rd, 4th pot and sees solid waste, urine, omit inside. Feeling disgusted by the filthy smell he asks women , 'what is this ugly joke? who are you?'

As she lifts her veil, sadhu frightens to see her. No hair on head, no glow on face, lustureless skin. She didn't eat anything for 7 days, her body was worn out.

His heart starts beating fast.

'Who are you? and where is that ravishing women I met last week. I came to meet her.'

She replies, 'It's me only maharaj. You asked for my Swaroop, so I kept it in front of you in those pots. This is my true form. When this was on me or inside me, you were finding me beautiful. Now, don't you find me beautiful?'

Like a lightning, sadhu understood what is happening.

*He says,' Mother, pl forgive me. I have diverted from my Path. I am grateful for saving me from falling me into trap of lust.'
"*

How blatantly the story shows the true mirror of human body. When an individual understands the temporary nature of body and its needs, he become aware and won't fall in trap of its needs mindlessly, rather he will exercise his free will to control or fulfil same. He becomes master than a servant of his needs.

Once, I received a call from somebody whose 'Akashik Records' has been accessed by me. He is a learned man and lives a life devoted to higher knowledge. A middle-aged, grounded, soft-spoken, and kind person. His records revealed his struggle with overcoming sexual entanglement, which is obstructing his spiritual evolvement. He told me this was his life's topmost secret not known to anyone but him. But now, since I knew the secret, he wanted to know why he is stuck?

He said 'I am happy in my marital relationship, wants to evolve spiritually, follow all that is needed to live a pious life and make every effort to practice' monogamy 'but then such situations, without any reason, happen that it becomes challenging for me to resist temptation, and unwantedly I go for it and regret. The cycle goes on, leaving me remorseful as I am unable to reach my spiritual goals. What could be the reason?'

It's revealed that in one of his lifetimes, he practiced polygamy. A lifetime of rich and wealthy person spent on material and physical enjoyment. The sexual energy exchanged among participating individuals created the most strong energetic imprints which inevitably get attracted to each other while in the body.

In one more such case, the person is devotedly following all that is needed to evolve. Still, then again, his entanglement with many other opposite energies as a part of his Tantrik Practices in previous lifetimes is causing hurdles in his growth. It takes many lifetimes to get over such karmic imprints.

Sooner or later, every soul wants to expand and evolve, free from all worldly entanglements and liberate. As you transcend and evolve, you raise your consciousness and your vibration, which then opens you up to see past the illusion and into the oneness. Let not your greed and temporary desires create a mountain of hurdles when you seek to reach Absolute.

Relationships

In the Sky, there is no distinction between East and West; People create distinctions out of their minds and then believe them to be true.- Buddha

Language is the most beautiful gift discovered by human being for itself. A word can make you laugh or tear you apart. It's a tool to communicate but used as a weapon. The wounds created by this weapon in relationships create imprints that go deep inside the mind and remain there for years. When we share our lives with so many others through bonds, differences in opinions are bound to happen. It's not possible that two people will agree with each other in any situation all the time. Every individual carries their sanskaras engraved in their mind, which seeks expression through a different situation. But when such differences of opinion happen in any relationship- personal or professional, instead of Discussion, Arguments happen only because of the control of EGO.

Arguments are about ME and MY view.

Discussions are about WE and OUR view.

Arguments happen to prove I am RIGHT...

Discussions happen to understand other's views, thus giving equal importance to others and arrive at the mutual output.

Arguments are the product of EGO and thus want EXCLUSIVITY.

Discussions are products of mutual trust, understanding and thus are INCLUSIVE.

Arguments are close-ended,

Healthy Discussions are open-ended.

The energy created in arguments is always negative and leaves soreness among people involved.

Healthy discussions create a positive environment and sow seeds for mutual bonds among participants.

Relationships

Let the power of language be used to express inner thoughts that bind and not to show our Ego that separates.

Whenever we know

ourselves spiritually,

we naturally know others too,

we know them in their spiritual essence, and then our relationships are deep, forever, and limitlessly meaningful. – Radhanath Swami

Anushka Kapse

Your Insight

🔻 *DROPLET FOURTEEN*

<u>Love</u>

Unless one dives deep in the ocean,

Depth won't be known...

Unless one climbs on the mountain,

Height won't be known.

Love will give you the experience of

Depth and Height at once.

Anushka Kapse

T*he name of 'Love' itself brings a twinkle in eyes and blush on cheeks...The feeling which everyone wants to experience but only a few could see it through its cloak, and more few scarcely experience it in entirety.*

One can hold the flower in hand, but who can catch the fragrance?

It needs to be experienced.

One has to experience love through the act of love. We all have the power to love and to be loved. Eternal Love is hidden under the layers of expectations, fears, hurt, sadness, Ego, desires, needs. The one who dares to remove these layers one by one starts experiencing the joy of love. Love starts to reveal itself. As he continues unwrapping these layers, he sees the enticing face of love and gets fascinated by its beauty. The time comes when he loves so much that it hurts.

Love hurts*...*

But if he continues unwrapping the layers, he will experience the magnetic pull of love within himself. In no time, he surrenders himself to the divine purity and becomes LOVE- the love that consumes the person who loves, become Love.

Love

Love is always pure, whether experienced in the relationship or outside.

Love doesn't have any relationship but only with itself.

The fine line between Lust and Love gets diminished when one experience that LOVE is our very own existence,

That 'We Are Love'.

The one who judges it by the earthly measures probably never experienced his own existence under the influence of Ego, insecurities, jealousy, and fears.

Love needs to be loved...

Love needs to be taken care of with love...

Love should be fulfilled with love...

A fertile land and proper care, turn a seed into a healthy tree.

A seed of Love once planted also needs to be nourished with affection and care else it will dry out eventually.

This is the reason why most of the love affair falls apart with time, as both the individuals forget to nourish it. The tree of love planted by both individuals needs

mutual effort so that they enjoy the fruits together. But this tree needs soil of longing, the water of mutual trust and respect, the air of faith, and energy of love.

You become a mother when you embody the energy of 'motherhood' in you, whether physically you are a man or a women.. that's why we see 'mother' in male deity (Mother Vitthal) also.

When this energy of 'motherhood' gets invoked, one doesn't need to teach how to express that love; it is so natural part of the being. A mother knows what her child wants; she is absorbed in her child, showering her entire love on him, a part of her which is inseparable. She feels that deep bonding within naturally.

True love doesn't need any external efforts to express. When one experiences the true essence of love, it becomes part of his being and thus gets expressed through his every act.

When someone gets angry, anger bursts out. When someone is happy, happiness spreads out. What is in, finds a way to come out without efforts ...

'Romantic love is a capitalist concept.'

Romantic love begins with wooing the other one through various ways available and possible. This is mostly the first step towards anyone's love life. The dreamy, passionate individuals experience the feeling of Love through the tool of romance. Many times, it remains at that level without further culminating into something deeper. The happiness of love is drawn through bodily senses, and thus it never gives fulfillment. Love remains in the physical realm. Everyone is in a hurry to extract happiness from others, and even a petty reason is enough to break the tender relationship and move forward to the next experience.

Many do get married as a result of this romantic love soon to realize there is no romance, neither love remained, but only the rituals of marriage. It needs time, patience, sensitivity, empathy, care, trust to build a long-lasting happy relationship.

Then there are those fortunate individuals who go through the roller coaster of life together, experiencing it together willingly. They are the ones whose romantic love has risen to the level of maturity, bringing happiness and contentment in life.

Once you establish in Love, you don't need a tool of romance.

Love is sufficient by itself.

When you start schooling, you need tools like pen, pencil, textbook, etc. to learn, but as you graduate and master the subject, you don't need these tools, but you carry the ESSENCE of your knowledge within you. Romantic love is a tool to begin the journey, but once you establish in love, you carry the ESSENCE within, and you don't need these tools in its entirety for happiness.

Love

I choose to Love you in silence...

For in silence I find no rejection,

I choose to Love you in loneliness...

For in loneliness no one owns you

but me,

I choose to adore you

from a distance...

For distance will shield me

from pain,

I choose to kiss you in the wind...

For the wind is gentler than my lips,

I choose to hold you in my dreams...

For in my dreams, you have no end

- *Rumi*

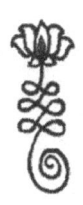

Your Insight

🌢 *DROPLET FIFTEEN*

Cosmic Roots

When the Root is Deep,

There is no reason

to Fear the Wind

- **African Proverb**

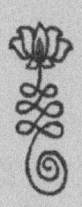

A flower bud, if we sow it in the same soil as the plant, will it bloom? **NO**

What could be the reason? The soil is supplying nourishment to the plant, then why is that same nourishment don't bloom the bud?

Is it because a bud is dependent on roots for nourishment, and it doesn't have the capacity to suck the same from the soil?

We can think of this as a layman who is dependent on a Guru for his blooming. True Guru is rooted to channelize cosmic guidance to seekers. A seeker who wants to bloom flower of his own life is happy to swing on this tree of a Guru by becoming a follower.

But if one wants to grow his tree, then he has to go deep below the surface, hiding from the material world, losing his own identity, developing a strong root structure that will nourish millions of buds. Their blooming is seen through these millions of buds.

A bud (seeker) enjoys worldly attention, praise, and gives happiness to others as long as it blooms.

Cosmic Roots

A root (enlightened being)provides nourishment to every bud that is grown on his tree.

The difference lies whether your bloomed bud is tender enough to dissolve in the divine, and your roots are vast enough to spread from limited existence to universal providence.

Everyone wants to get identified with something to feel secure. The tree of our life needs to be rooted somewhere. Various communities, religions, societies got created due to this need of the human mind to get identified, to be attached to something. This identity then goes to minuscule as gender identity, professional identity, interest/hobby based identity. This, we also called like-minded people coming together.

Known things make us feel secure.

If such identities flourish healthily, allowing other personalities also to blossom and live, there wouldn't have been so much violence and unrest in the world. But the roots of these identities are nourished by hatred, self-importance, power control, and thus these trees reap fruits that are prejudiced and ignorant to reality.

When someone dares to rip off these conditioned and prejudiced identities and get rooted in THAT which is beyond any qualities, identity, which is ABSOLUTELY ABSOLUTE, the UNKNOWN, he will find TRUTH of Our Existence.

The unknown will make you fearless when you identify yourself with him.

In this cosmos, on a Giant Tree of Life, there are multiple big and small trees, plants, shrubs all intertwined to the cosmic root. We, as a human being, sometimes live like a bud and sometimes like a root to others.

We are both - a bud and a root.

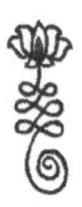

◆ *DROPLET SIXTEEN*

Himalaya

Deep valleys and
rugged mountain,
misty meadows and
snow-capped mountain,
shades of green and
the palette of gold,
Himalaya appeared to me
as my beloved ...
As my soul soaked deep
in the serenity;
he opened his hidden treasure,

The magical feeling of immense love blossomed within;

and like a bumblebee caught drinking nectar from the flower,

I caught in the divinity of his majesty Himalaya.

As he threw open his arms,

I just surrendered,

Like a lover,

eternally surrendered

to his beloved.

Himalaya

Majestic Himalayas...

If you experience it once, I bet you will want to go there again and again.

What is so special about this seemingly young mountain ranges of India that sages, seers, and aspirants want to hide in it.

Is it the beauty? Naaaa

You will find many more beautiful, more vast, expansive mountains across the globe than Himalaya.

But He is different.

The Air that touches the mountain brings the fragrance of deep love with it. The energy exuberated in the valley touches you on the deeper level of your being.

As Om SwamiJi said, 'Just as silicon valley has necessary resources that support start ups, Himalaya has resources that support seekers.'.

Since ancient times thousands of seers and sages had meditated in deeper Himalayas, leaving behind the energy of their spiritual fleets. Every year millions travel for pilgrimage in the Himalayas carrying so much devotion and reverence in their heart, chanting the names of divine.

It is this energy that makes the Himalaya so unique and stands apart from others.

Let me share a story :

"Once there was a farmer who discovered that he had lost his watch in the farm. It was not an ordinary watch because it had sentimental value for him.

After searching the hay for a long while, he gave up and called the help of a group of children playing outside the barn. He promised them that the person who found it would be rewarded.

Hearing this, the children hurried inside the barn, went through and around the hay but still could not find the watch. Just when the farmer was about to give up looking for his watch, a little boy went up to him and asked to be given another chance.

The farmer looked at him and thought, "Why not.? After all, this kid looks sincere enough."

So the farmer sent the little boy back in the barn. After a while, the little boy came out

Himalaya

with the watch in his hand. The farmer was happy and surprised, and so he asked the boy how he succeeded where the rest had failed.

The boy replied, "I did nothing but sit on the ground and listen. In the silence, I heard the ticking of the watch and just looked for it in that direction."

The soul always knows what to do to heal itself. The challenge is to silence the mind."

Himalaya offers that silence.

And in silence and solitude of your heart, it will whisper the music of this cosmos just for you to enjoy and dance, to be you.

Let the song be enjoyed.

Let the silence be heard.

Anushka Kapse

Your Insight

_____

_____

_____

_____

_____

_____

_____

◆ DROPLET SEVENTEEN

Pot

फिरत्या चाकावरती देसी मातीला आकार,

विठ्ठला तू वेडा कुंभार ||

माती, पाणी, उजेड, वारा, तूच मिसळसी सर्व पसारा

आभाळच मग ये आकारा, तुझ्या घटांच्या उतरंडीला

नसे अंत ना पार ||

घटाघटाचे रूप आगळे, प्रत्येकाचे दैव वेगळे

*तुझ्या विना हे कोणा न कळे, मुखी कुणाच्या पडते लोणी
कुणा मुखी अंगार ||*

तूच घडविसी, तूच फोडीशी, कुरवाळिसि तू, तूच जोडीशी

न कळे यातून काय सांधींशी, देसी डोळे परी निर्मिसी

तया पुढे अंधार || G.D.Madgulkar

Translation: O lord vitthala, you are a mad potter who gives shape to soil on a revolving wheel. When you mix soil, water, light, and air, the magnificent space thus gets created, and the Creation has no start and end. Every pot that you have created has a different destiny that only you know; some eat butter, some get burn. You create, you destroy, you care, you join.. we don't understand what you achieve by giving eyes but no vision.

When a child cries for his mother, he has been distracted by giving toys to play or keep him engaged by trying to make him laugh by making faces or sounds, by telling stories. A child does get temporarily distracted, plays with a toy for some time, but again starts crying for mother. The cycle keeps repeating till he sees his mother and the joy, the bliss, the fulfillment he gets by her love, makes him throw away all that has distracted him. He then just wants to be played in the mother's lap and soak in her love, feeling eternally happy.

Our soul too cries for Love of supreme soul (Divine Mother) as it feels the pain of separation when it is embodied. He then offered various toys (MAYA) to play with.

Pot

Toy of Ego,

Toy of material wealth,

Toy of Relationships,

***Toy of Desires**... so on*

Since Creation, evolution is ever happening. Human species is considered to be the most evolved, and human life is the most precious gift given to us. But still, the majority of people live a miserable life in the human body by involving themselves in toys.

Life evolved from minerals to plants to animals to humans, and with this, there was a continuous evolvement of the brain. The lower brain (reptilian) controls our fear, anger, sex, hunger, and basic well-being. The living organism was operating through the lower brain, and thus survival animal instinct was at the root of human existence. As evolvement happened, the upper neo-cortex or monkey chattering brain got prominence in human existence. It evolved our logical, analytical, thinking power. With this, human beings started moving away from its original nature. And as the mind and it's tendencies started using the brainpower only to exercise control over others, to fulfill greed and lust, the world became a place fully consummated by darkness.

The eternal soul got cladded with layers of envy, power, lust, ego, jealousy, pride, violence, anger. The light of the human soul got covered by these vices, and the virtues of love, compassion, kindness, empathy got buried deep inside the human heart.

If we immerse a pot in water, what will you say: Pot is in water or water is in the pot?

An ignorant will say either of it, but wise one knows it's Pot that is separating the water, thus creating an illusion of external and internal water, once the pot is broken, external and internal merges.

This is the dual and non-dual nature of our existence. The supreme, omniscient Absolute (Paramatma) is all around us. Our body which encompasses the soul (jivatma), creates the illusion of separation. As we live and experience the life here on earth, the impressions thus gathered either increase or decrease the illusion of this separation. Each lifetime is an opportunity given to us to reduce the illusionary gap between jivatma and Paramatma. However, human being under the influence of Maya creates layers around the soul and goes away from the supreme being.

When dust accumulates on a pot, you will simply wipe it with clean cloth effortlessly. If it's dirtier, you may use detergent and water, but for tougher stains, you will need to use specific potent remedies to bring back the original shine.

The ultimate goal of Human Life is 'Liberation' 'Enlightenment' 'Self Realization.'

As I read :

"

Liberation' is not 'Enlightenment' and

'Understanding' is not 'Self Realization.

"

The difference is the same as getting a 'Degree' by writing an exam and actually applying the acquired knowledge to get the 'Experience.'

There is a conception that to get liberation, one needs to leave every worldly thing and retire to Himalaya. There are thousands in this world who renunciate everything in search of Truth, but very few can get hold of it. Many understand it, but the experience still evades them.

Getting enlightened is purely a result of 'Grace.'

As I read :

"

There are hundreds who live a monastic life but couldn't overcome their carnal desires and there are many who will appear living a worldly life but are free from attachments.

"

We are the only species that has offered the gift of Free Will. It is this special gift that empowers us to experience other realities beyond senses.

As Osho explains:

"

The 7 valleys or 7 heavens or 7 chakras are rungs of a Ladder which connects us to different realities.

Pot

We, as human beings, have offered this tool to liberate ourselves and return HOME.

The 1st rung is of survival instinct

The 2nd rung is of sexuality and creativity

The 3rd rung is of self-power, self-goal.

The 4th rung is pycho-spiritual

The 5th rung is of expression

The 6th rung is of seeing

The 7th rung is of Divine connection.

A rung is called a Rung only when it is part of a ladder. Human being gets entangled in rung and forget about ladder and lifetime after lifetime lives a life, feeling separated and miserable.

"

Lifetime after lifetime, we live life mostly governed by three lower rungs. These are also called 'Lower worlds'; animals live through these worlds of physical pleasures enjoyed through physical senses. When the consciousness operates from the human aspect of the living being of 'awareness' *and 'power of discrimination,' he lives a life governed by the 4th rung, which is 'Transition World.' He gets an opportunity to move from 'Lower World' to 'Upper World.' To experience life beyond physical senses.*

We have come here on earth to learn something, to get experience.

When it's for learning, the experience is external, and the outcome when internalized becomes WISDOM. Such wisdom then becomes our inherited nature and a part of US.

It's through experience, one gets WISDOM, and through WISDOM, one can draw happiness again and again.

A mountain will not understand its strength unless faced by the storm. Mountain will not have any or minor effect of the storm on it, but the strong wind might have created havoc on ground life below.

One can know its own worth in challenging situations. He can analyze his behavior during a crisis and understand his personal mental, emotional, spiritual strength, and weakness. This introspection

Pot

will lead to accepting oneself with all flaws and gifts.

A wise person will not get swayed away by his strength; neither feel inferior for flaws. He will be composed and balanced. Don't flight when challenges barge in, its time to check your inner self.

If you want to experience the light of your soul, you will need to be aware of the dirt that is accumulated on your soul. The challenging and stressful situations or relationships are there to shake you up so that you will take corrective measures. Still, unfortunately, due to ignorance, we end up creating more and more thick layers around our soul and move farther from absolute reality.

Remember, Cream is formed when Milk is BOILED and then STILLED ...

The more the boiled and stilled is Milk, the THICKER will be the cream.

Meditation, self-contemplation, prayers, social work, simple living, invoking devotion, and compassion for others will help us in the non-accumulation of dirt.

Anushka Kapse

If you want to know the Creator,

Love and Serve its Creation,

Grace will bound to come.

The awakening of the soul to its bondage and its effort to stand up and assert itself – this is called life.

-Swami Vivekanand

◆ *DROPLET EIGHTEEN*

INNER LOTUS

As the Lotus rises on its stalk

unsoiled by mud and water,

So the wise one speaks of peace

and is unstained by

the opinions of the world.

-Buddha

There was a merchant who was dealing in trading of cloth bags. He was using a small box to keep his money and used to carry this box in a cloth bag whenever he used to go for business dealings. By just holding the bag, he used to feel very calm and energetic, making him more confident of getting the business deal he wanted. It was his priced possession. Once, his servant gave him another similar bag keeping his money box inside. Not noticing anything, the merchant went out to meet regular vendors.

But he was very uncomfortable and felt irritated throughout the day. He was having headaches due to a specific pungent smell. He looked around for the origin of the smell. As he picked up his bag, he realized it's not his regular bag and smell is coming from it.

When he returned home, he asks his servant,

"where is my bag, and whose bag you gave me today?"

Servant gets frightened and lies,

"I couldn't find an old bag, so I gave you another similar looking bag."

Inner Lotus

Merchant becomes furious and demands,

"Give me my old bag; else you are fired."

Now, the servant gets worried as he has mixed his old bag with many other similar bags for recycling.

How to find his master's bag?

There was a wise man in that village. The servant told him about the bag and was hopefully looking at him for a solution. The wise man asks him to get all cloth bags in which his master's bag was mixed. The servant keeps all bags in front of a wise man. All were precisely the same bags-in shape, in size, in color. The wise man looks carefully and asks the servant

"your master was using this bag for what?"

'To carry money." replies the servant.

Hmmm, the wise man starts thinking.

He then asks, "'Were he carrying only money in the bag? "

"yes," said the servant.

"Was he keeping his money directly in the bag?" wise man probes further.

"Yes', the servant replies irritatedly.

But then blurted, "No, no, my master used to keep money in a box. That box was very dear to him. "

Taking this clue, the wise man starts smelling each man. Soon, he shortlists three bags and says,

"Out of these three bags, one bag is smelling of flowers, another of fish and 3rd is of sandalwood. As your master is so particular to find THAT bag, it must be valuable to him. Take the 3rd bag and give it to your master."

The servant was happy and did as instructed by a wise man.

Master takes a close look at the bag and then SMELLS, and a BIG smile flashes on his face.

"Yes, this is my bag. The money box is of SANDALWOOD, and for years I am keeping it in this bag, so my bag also smells like sandalwood. This fragrance offers me peace and a feeling of goodwill, so I always carry it with me. Don't you ever dare to change it or throw it. This bag is valuable to me, just like my Sandalwood Box."

The story ends here.

What is the value of an ordinary cloth bag? But when it was associated with a precious thing like Sandalwood, even it became valuable.

*This is the power of **ASSOCIATION**.*

Consciously or unconsciously, we reflect the qualities of other people with whom we associate ourselves. If the association is worthy, even a drop of water becomes PEARL else it gets lost in the MUD. Our association shapes our belief system, influence our behavior, develop positive or negative habits.

When our association gets strengthened to a level where it starts controlling us, it becomes Surrender.

*One of the definitions of **Surrender** is willful acceptance and yielding to a dominating force and their will.*

You become what you have surrendered yourself to.

If your surrender is to money, you will become MONEY everyone wants to USE.

If your surrender is to success, you will become a SUCCESS; everyone wants to ENJOY.

If your surrender is to wisdom, you will become WISDOM; everyone wants to LISTEN.

If your surrender is to compassion, empathy, love, you will become LOVE; everyone wants to SOAK.

If your surrender is to the universe, you will become UNIVERSE; everyone wants to FOLLOW.

The spiritual knowledge of Self-Realization was kept hidden for thousands of years from the layman. The sacred knowledge used to pass on through Guru-Disciple traditions. Later on, through written records and verbal communication, folklore this knowledge used to reach ordinary people. As society advanced, hidden knowledge became available to anyone who wishes to learn it. And in today's time, due to technological advancement, this knowledge is so readily available that it is losing its real value.

When gathered information is understood, it becomes knowledge, and when such knowledge is internalized, it becomes wisdom.[2] The current era is of Information overload. You will get all that is needed, and most of the time, all that is not needed information by the click of a button.

We must understand the deeper meaning of such profound knowledge that is available to us. Never than before, we have such a tremendous opportunity to know our true nature.

Human beings must utilize this opportunity and raise individual consciousness to a higher level. We must disassociate ourselves from Lust, Anger, Greed, Attachment, Ego, Passion, Jealousy, Fear, Hate, Shame, and strengthen our association with Humility, Sacrifice,

---

[2] *Taken from Om Swami ji's talk.*

Compassion, Patience, forgiveness, kindness, freedom. As we establish more and more in positive virtue, we become Self Purified, moving closer, and closer to our ultimate nature.

We know the story of 'The Ugly Duckling' in our childhood. It goes like this,

In a pond, many beautiful ducklings were swimming happily. But there was this one ugly looking duckling, and everyone used to laugh on him, bully him, tease him. Nobody used to play with him. The ugly duckling was feeling very sad and lonely. One night, he leaves this pond and starts wandering in search of a nicer family to stay. But as his duck family, he could't live with geese and human family too.

Meanwhile, he was growing larger; his feathers were coming in. But he was feeling sorrowful. Once as he sat by the water's edge, he saw the most beautiful bird family-Swan. But fearing rejection, he didn't even dare to join. Suddenly, a swan glided through the water over to ugly duckling.

"My, my! Your feathers are the whitest I have ever seen. How they shine in the sun!" the swan exclaimed to the ugly duckling.

Confused, the ugly duckling wandered to the water and peered at his reflection.

He was a beautiful white swan with a long and elegant neck. "

The story ends here.

We see and treat ourselves as per our association with our immediate surroundings. Even though we are that beautiful swan in the story, we made to believe that we are ducks. Our true potential gets lost in believing others lie till the time we don't find our eternal nature. But you need to search and search and search to find your SELF. Once you know that you are that beautiful Swan (Universe), you are HOME.

As Om Swami Ji said, 'There are two journeys which are done alone. 1st is the journey of Death, and 2nd is your Spiritual journey.

You must walk on your spiritual path even if you feel there is nobody to walk with you, even if nothing about your environment is supportive to you except your own longing for Truth. Everyone has a different blooming season, and if your inner flower wants to bloom, provide it with required nourishment. Remember that you are never alone on this path; keep faith that you will always be provided help by unseen forces of the universe.

In current time, False is so confidently and cleverly wrapped as Truth, that it is impossible to separate 'Absolute Truth' from 'Seemingly True Truth.' How to establish oneself in Absolute then? Who to depend on knowing Truth in kali yuga?

It's your inner intelligence.

Inner Lotus

Lotus flower is a sacred flower considered as the symbol of Purity, Enlightenment, Transcendence, Knowledge in India. Almost all God/Goddesses are shown holding this sacred flower or sitting/standing on it.

The flower rises from murky water, untouched by its impure surrounding. It rises above in its 'Purity' and shines in full glory.

The lotus seed needs MUD and SUNLIGHT to bloom. Our soul, when it enters the MUD of the physical world, too, gets an opportunity to blossom to its original glory. But till the time SUNLIGHT of inner knowledge doesn't break through the murky water, the soul remains in darkness. It enjoys the MUD, unaware of its potential.

When even a single ray of sunlight reaches to it, the petals of its awakening start opening till the time in BLOOMS entirely in the bright SUNLIGHT of Sacred Inner Knowledge.

Anushka Kapse

Let the SUNLIGHT reach you.

Let the INNER LOTUS bloom.

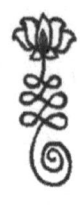

About the Author

An Engineer by education, Anushka Kapse, is an intuitive Akashik Records Reader, Past Life Regression Therapist, Reiki Master, and Energy healer by choice. She specializes in guiding individuals to know their true self and evolve. The scientific mind blended in Spiritual wisdom is her key strength. Before diving deep into spirituality, she was running a successful Engineering Consulting business. At present, she devotes herself to help and heal others to find their true self and lead a more balanced life. She is fortunate to be a disciple of a Living Himalayan Guru.

She is an avid reader and a meditator, and loves singing and traveling when not busy serving underprivileged children through her NGO 'Metta Foundation.'

She will be happy to hear from you on::

eternalyou18@gmail.com

www.eternalyou.org
www.mettafoundationindia.org

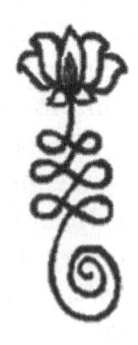

Throughout the book, you must have noticed above symbol.

*This is a Buddhist Spiritual Symbol called **'Unalome'**. It represents life's path toward Enlightment.*

The spiral represents our struggle with life and upward path for self Realization.

Made in the USA
Las Vegas, NV
30 January 2021